BASKETBALL LEGENDS

Kareem Abdul-Jabbar

Charles Barkley

Larry Bird

Wilt Chamberlain

Clyde Drexler

Julius Erving

Patrick Ewing

Anfernee Hardaway

Grant Hill

Magic Johnson

Michael Jordan

Jason Kidd

Reggie Miller

Hakeem Olajuwon

Shaquille O'Neal

Scottie Pippen

David Robinson

Dennis Rodman

CHELSEA HOUSE PUBLISHERS

BASKETBALL LEGENDS

CHARLES BARKLEY.

Sean Dolan

Introduction by
Chuck Daly

CHELSEA HOUSE PUBLISHERS
New York • Philadelphia

Produced by Daniel Bial and Associates
New York, New York

Picture research by Alan Gottlieb
Cover illustration by Bill Vann

3 5 7 9 8 6 4 2

Library of Congress Cataloging-in-Publication Data

Dolan, Sean.
       Charles Barkley / Sean Dolan.
            p. cm. -- (Basketball legends)
         Includes bibliographical references and index.
          ISBN 0-7910-2433-4
      1. Barkley, Charles, 1963-   Basketball players--United
     States--Biography. I. Title. II. Series
     GV884.B28D65 1996
     796.323'092--dc20

                                                    [B]95-30124
                                                          CIP
                                                          AC

CONTENTS

BECOMING A
BASKETBALL LEGEND

Chuck Daly

What does it take to be a basketball superstar? Two of the three things it takes are easy to spot. Any great athlete must have excellent skills and tremendous dedication. The third quality needed is much harder to define, or even put in words. Others call it leadership or desire to win, but I'm not sure that explains it fully. This third quality relates to the athlete's thinking process, a certain mentality and work ethic. One can coach athletic skills, and while few superstars need outside influence to help keep them dedicated, it is possible for a coach to offer some well-timed words in order to keep that athlete fully motivated. But a coach can do no more than appeal to a player's will to win; how much that player is then capable of ensuring victory is up to his own internal workings.

In recent times, we have been fortunate to have seen some of the best to play the game. Larry Bird, Magic Johnson, and Michael Jordan had all three components of superstardom in full measure. The brought their teams to numerous championships, and made the players around them better. (They also made their coaches look smart.)

I myself coached a player who belongs in that class, Isiah Thomas, who helped leader the Detroit Pistons to consecutive NBA crowns. Isiah is not tall—he's just over six feet—but he could do whatever he wanted with the ball. And what he wanted to do most was lead and win.

All the players I mentioned above and those whom this series will chronicle are tremendously gifted athletes, but for the most part, you can't play professional basketball at all unless you have excellent skills. And few players get to stay on their team unless they are willing to dedicate themselves to improving their talents even more, learning about their opponents, and finding a way to join with their teammates and win.

It's that third element that separates the good player from the superstar, the memorable players from the legends of the game. Superstars known when to take over the game. If the situation calls for a defensive stop, the superstars stand up and do it. If the situation calls for a big shot, they want the ball. They don't want the ball simply because of their own glory or ego. Instead they know—and their teammates know—-that they are the ones who can deliver, regardless of the pressure.

The words "legend" and "superstar" are often tossed around without real meaning. Taking a hard look at some of those who truly can be classified as "legends" can provide insight into the things that brought them to that level. All of them developed their legacy over numerous season of play, even if certain games will always stand out in the memories of those who saw them. Those games typically featured amazing feats of all-around play. No matter how great the fans thought the superstars, the players were capable yet of surprising them, their opponents, and occasionally even themselves. The desire to win took over, and with their dedication and athletic skills already in place, they were capable of the most astonishing achievements.

CHUCK DALY, most recently the head coach of the New Jersey Nets, guided the Detroit Pistons to two straight NBA championships, in 1989 and 1990. He earned a gold medal as coach of the 1992 U.S. Olympic basketball team—the so-called "Dream Team"— and was inducted into the Pro Basketball Hall of Fame in 1994.

1

A MOST UNUSUAL PLAYER

He is a walking contradiction—or, perhaps more properly put, a running, leaping, rebounding contradiction. Charles Barkley, says Jerry West, a Hall-of-Fame guard as a player and today (as the general manager of the Los Angeles Lakers) one of professional basketball's shrewdest judges of talent, is "perhaps the most unusual player in the history of the NBA [National Basketball Association]." West is referring specifically to the unlikely combination of physical attributes and skills that Barkley brings to bear on a game of basketball, but he might just as well be speaking about the combustible mixture of character traits that, along with his superior ability and unconcealed drive, has made Barkley perhaps the most unpredictable, consistent, charismatic, infuriating, volatile, frustrating, colorful, and exciting player in the game today.

When he comes out on court, Charles

Charles Barkley leads a fast break at the 1991 All-Star Game. Barkley was named Most Valuable Player of the game.

Barkley fights for position to grab a rebound away from Horace Grant of the Chicago Bulls in the 1993 playoffs.

Barkley makes a strange first impression. Most players in the NBA are graceful-looking and lean. Barkley, at just 6' 4 1/2", is short by the standards of professional basketball and especially undersized for the position he plays—power forward. Almost all other power forwards have carefully-sculpted physiques. Barkley is phenomenally strong, but his upper body lacks definition. In a league of long, lithe physical specimens, he appears not just short but almost squat. While stars such as Michael Jordan and Julius Erving enjoyed enormously long wingspans and huge hands that enabled them to palm the basketball off the dribble and wave it about in one hand like a grapefruit, Barkley's arms are comparatively short and his hands small, requiring him to cup the ball, or, more often, grasp it with both hands when rising to the rim.

Yet Barkley can fly as well as any basketball player alive. "I think God is in my body," Barkley has often said, and it seems as good an explanation as any for what he has been able to accomplish. Seemingly undersized and over-stuffed at the same time, Barkley has nonethe-less proven himself one of the most dominant, explosive forces in the game's history. In action, the body that seems so ill-suited for basketball is transformed, and Barkley becomes the proto-type for a new kind of basketball player.

"There will never be another 6'4" guy who can accomplish what I've accomplished. Ever. Ever," Barkley said to a reporter from the *New York Times* in 1991. Every game pits him against players who are anywhere from two to eight inches taller. Height is less important for small forwards, but he is even too short, by con-ventional standards, to play there. The shortest basketball players are the guards—and there have been many guards taller than Barkley. But he clearly is too bulky to play at the guard posi-tion.

So Barkley would seem to be at a disadvan-tage, but it is his opponents who pay the price. "Height is overrated," he says; "I've played with a lot of bad tall players." Coaches spend hours examining film and dissecting personnel in an attempt to create "mismatches"—finding ways their players are stronger than their counter-parts on the opposing team. This makes Barkley the most valuable of players, for he brings his team a favorable mismatch virtually every single time he steps on the court. "I'm too quick for the big guys, and too strong for the smaller guys," he says.

No player who approaches him in terms of power and strength—and there may not be a stronger player in the league—is anywhere near quick enough to guard him, especially since he possesses extremely advanced ballhandling skills for a power forward. At the same time, anyone quick enough to stay with Barkley is seldom strong enough to keep from being overwhelmed "in the paint," which is where "Sir Charles" earns his living, converting shots off the offensive boards, posting up, and drawing fouls. "If I was seven feet tall, I'd be illegal in three states," he proudly proclaims.

The result, said Barkley in 1991, is that "can't nobody on planet Earth guard me. Nobody. I mean that." The numbers bear him out: nine times an All Star, nine times a first or second All-NBA team selection, once a Most Valuable Player. For his career Barkley is the league's fifth-highest active scorer (23.3 points per game), its second-most accurate shooter (.562 percent), and, at a height more befitting a guard, one of its very best rebounders, averaging almost 12 per game over the course of his career. Of the game's top ten active career scorers, Barkley takes by far the fewest shots per game. Combined with his ability to draw fouls from overmatched opponents, this means that he scores more points on fewer shots than any other player; of all the game's great scorers, Barkley is by far the most efficient. Yet statistics provide a most inadequate measure of the man, for, like any legendary creature, Barkley must be seen to be believed.

Barkley is a quick leaper rather than an exceptionally high one. He does not need to gather himself in order to elevate and can jump several times in the course of a short span in which other players might only get up once. "Any knucklehead can score," he is fond of proclaiming. What thrills him is coming down with the basketball following an errant shot, when every other player on the court, most of them taller, is equally desperate to gain control of it.

"Nothing in the game gives me as much of a rush as the feeling I get when I grab an offensive rebound over two or three guys in the final three minutes of a game," he explained in *Outrageous*, his 1992 autobiography. His rebounding technique is unusual, as one might expect from so singular a player. More often than not, he simply ignores the proverbial coaching wisdom that exhorts rebounders to first "box out" their counterparts on the opposing team. Secure that his strength and "low center of gravity"—by low center of gravity, I mean he's got a big butt," explained Mychal Thompson of the Los Angeles Lakers—makes it impossible for others to move him. He instead

Barkley may need two hands in order to dunk, but other players still prefer to get out of his way when he has a clear shot at the basket.

concentrates on simply being the first player off the floor after the basketball, as well as the last, if need be. His technique is called "Just Go Get the Damn Ball," he says. "I pursue the basketball. Jumping is one thing; pursuit is another thing entirely. The bottom line is that the player who wants the ball more than anybody else on the floor will come down with it." Not surprisingly, he has led the league in overall rebounding once, and in offensive rebounds three times.

Having rebounded the ball at the defensive end, Barkley will often ignite the fast break not, as basketball custom would dictate, by making an outlet pass to a guard, but by turning, putting the ball on the floor, and dribbling upcourt himself at full tilt. There is no grander sight in the game than Barkley with the ball leading the break, moving impossibly fast for a man his size, going around his back with a high dribble at midcourt to elude a defender, barreling toward the hoop as seemingly out-of-control as a runaway truck, yet able to finish the break with a delicate, perfectly-placed bounce pass to a teammate, or a rimrocking two-handed dunk. For the spectator, the sensation is the strangely exhilarating one of disaster narrowly averted, like watching, from some safe vantage point, an overloaded freight train rocket through the stop signal at a junction and successfully negotiate a hairpin curve at full throttle.

Those foolish enough to stand in his way when Barkley gathers a full head of steam are often left scattered like bowling pins. At the 1984 Olympic trials, Joe Dumars tried to get an offensive foul called on Barkley. "That was the first time I'd ever been around anybody that big who could be that explosive," recalls Dumars, then a guard for McNeese State and since a perennial All-Star player with the Detroit Pistons. "I was just amazed when I first saw Charles, how cat-quick and how agile he was. . . . As for taking that charge, I was young and silly. That was the last time I took a charge on him. Ever. At the time I thought it was admirable; now that I look back on it, it was pure foolishness. Pure, pure foolishness."

Despite all the statistical achievements and moments of on-court brilliance, Barkley has yet to receive his true due as a player. His estimable game now often seems to be in danger of being overshadowed by his endlessly entertaining, maddeningly contradictory public persona.

A perennial league leader in technical fouls, a participant in two of the most spectacular brawls in NBA history, Barkley has cursed, made obscene gestures at, hit, and even spat upon fans. Yet he remains one of the NBA's premier box-office draws. An extremely popular commercial spokesman, he pointedly reminds young fans again and again that he should not be regarded as a role model, yet has been known to take to the floor with wristbands inscribed with the initials of terminally ill children whom he visits, without publicity, in the hospital. Regarded by some observers as obnoxious and loud-mouthed, he is respected by his teammates for his generosity, especially toward first-year and marginal players.

"I Don't Mind Being a Jerk" is what Barkley called the first chapter of his autobiography, but those who know him suggest that the truth is more complicated, as indicated by the fact that the book's prologue is entitled "An Apology."

"Charles is the exact opposite of most

In the 1992 Olympic Games, Barkley played on the "Dream Team." Many said he was the most impressive player on a squad that also featured Michael Jordan and Magic Johnson.

modern athletes," explains Dave Coskey, the former public relations director for the 76ers. "Most of these guys are jerks who want you to think they're nice guys. But Charles is a genuinely nice guy who wants you to think he's a jerk." The first to defend his teammates, yet also often the first to criticize them, Barkley prides himself on his willingness to speak the truth as he sees it, regardless of consequence. Yet he insisted that he had been misquoted in his own autobiography when some remarks he made there drew heavy criticism.

"I scare people," he's said. "I'm big and I'm black. That's double-scary." The years of banging with giants under the basket has taken its claim on Barkley's health. "My body's disintegrating," he explains while reciting a long list of injuries, both acute and chronic. "Something always hurts." Some days, he is unable to get out of bed without assistance, and he no longer can play all out for an entire season.

Yet winning is no less important to him than when he was a younger, healthier player. "Winning is the only thing that makes it worthwhile," he explains. The physical pain he endures, he says, is thus not the hardest part of being Charles Barkley in the twilight of his career, still searching for that elusive championship ring. "The hardest part for me," he says, "is the pressure to be Charles Barkley every night."

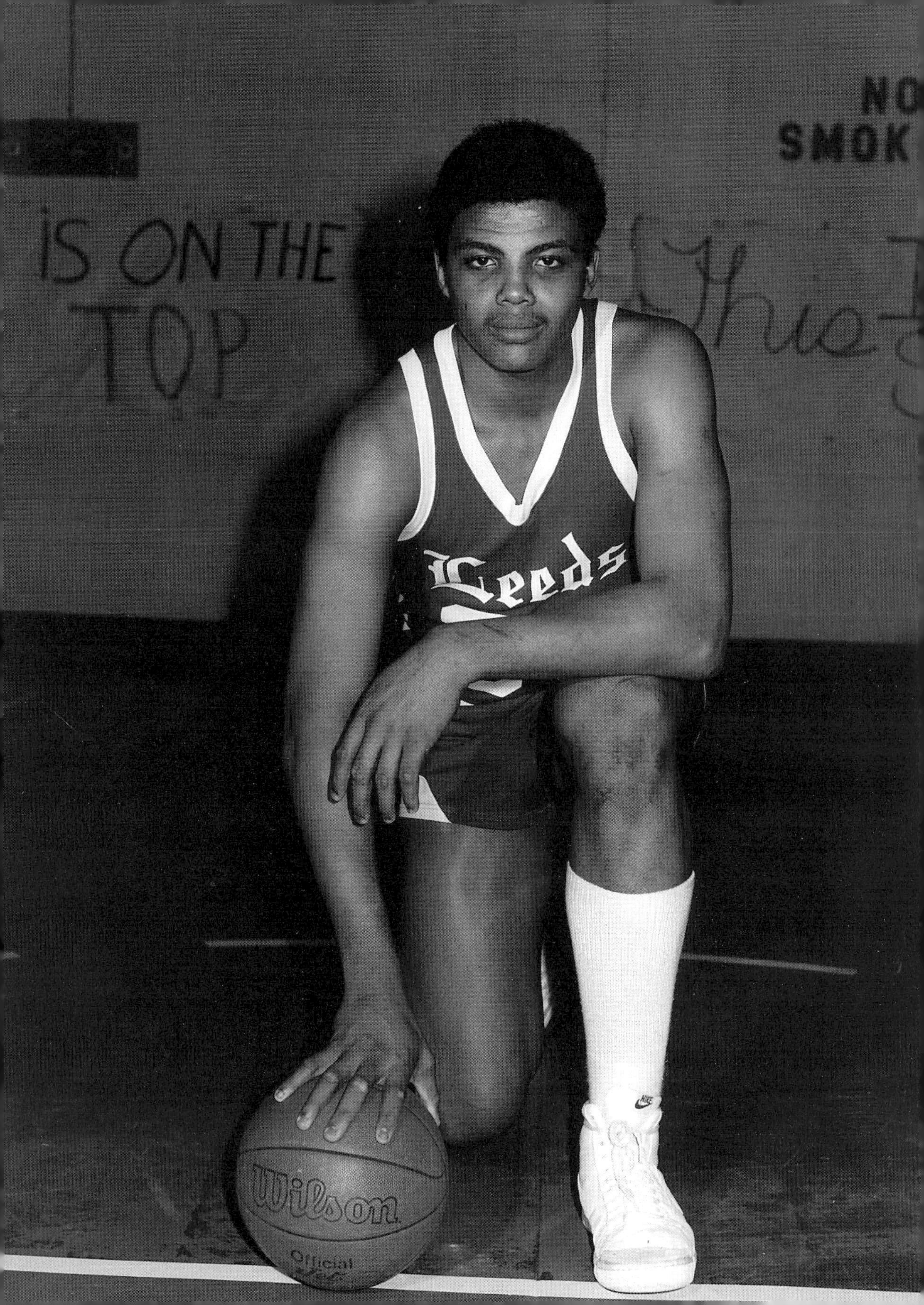
NO
SMOK
IS ON THE
TOP
Leeds
Wilson
Official

2

MAMA'S BOY

"**G**rowing up black in a single-parent home does not have to be a damn death sentence. Because it wasn't for me." Barkley grew up in a public housing project without a father, sometimes in the absence of much adult supervision at all (his mother had to work two different jobs to make ends meet). "Anyone," he believes, "can raise themselves out of their condition if they concentrate on getting an education, working hard, and understanding what it takes to be successful."

It all began for Charles Wade Barkley on February 20, 1963, in Leeds, Alabama, a small town of several thousand people in the central part of the state, about 15 miles from Birmingham. He was not an especially large baby, just six pounds twelve ounces at birth, and he was so anemic that he needed blood transfusions for the first six months of his life.

Even as a kid, Charles Barkley was always a hard worker on the basketball court—as a knee full of scars shows clearly.

His mother, Charcey Mae Gaither, later described herself as "just a baby having a baby" at the time of the birth of her oldest son. The description, she said, applied as well to her husband, Frank Barkley. The two of them had graduated together from Moton High School in Leeds just nine months earlier, in May 1962. At about the same time, Charcey Mae became pregnant, and the two were married in June. Eight months later, Charles was born. Thirteen months later, Frank left.

The responsibility of marriage and providing for a family, with no college education and few marketable job skills, proved more than Frank was willing or able to deal with. "Like me," remembered his wife, "he was young and untrained, not for skilled work nor for marriage, and he simply couldn't cope with the responsibilities of fatherhood."

Charles would not see his father again until he was nine years old, by which time Frank was remarried and living in southern California with his new wife and four more children. "For much of my life," Charles recalled in *Outrageous,* "I had no image of my father. He left us when I was only a year old, and until I saw him again when I was nine, I had no real idea of who he was, what type of person he was, nothing."

Fortunately for Charles, his mother had inherited a large amount of the pride and feistiness that her own mother, Johnnie Mae Gaither, possessed in such abundance.

Charles and his mother moved in with Johnnie Mae and her second husband, Adolphus Edwards. The four of them shared a one-bedroom apartment in a government housing project in a neighborhood called Moton, but the extended family made up in closeness what it lacked in space and money.

Charcey Mae worked in the Leeds High School cafeteria and as a maid, going straight from one job to the other. Johnnie Mae worked in a meat-packing factory and later became a nurse. Adolphus Edwards, meanwhile, according to Charcey Mae, "became the most important man in Charles's life, a father figure for a boy who had been abandoned by his own flesh and blood." Charles took to calling Edwards "Little Daddy," and even after Edwards and Johnnie Mae were divorced, he and the boy spent much time together. Often, Charles would spend the weekend with Edwards at his home. "Charles was his heart," Charcey Mae explained.

Everyone who knew the family, however, agreed that in temperament and personality Barkley most took after his grandmother. "They've got ways so much alike that it's just unreal," Charcey Mae told the sportswriter Roy S. Johnson, who worked with Barkley on *Outrageous.* "I used to say to Granny, 'Momma, I know I had Charles, but sometimes I don't know whether he's your child or mine.'" The characteristic that Charles and his grandmother most obviously share is a willful outspokenness. "With her," Charcey Mae says, referring to her

Two "peacekeepers" and their attack dogs keep an eye on a civil rights demonstration. Birmingham, Alabama, was the site of many early protests in the Civil Rights Movement.

mother, "what comes up from the gut just about comes out her mouth. So I guess Charles gets that from his grandmother. . . . Anyone who knows my mother and Charles will say they're the same way. She won't bite her tongue. If she wants to tell you something, she will. She'll say, 'If I hurt your feelings, I'm sorry, but I meant what I said.'"

Barkley confirms the likeness. "Granny and I are like twins," he says. "We're both determined, stubborn, and very aggressive at whatever we set out to do. We both believe in hard work and in getting out of life exactly what we put into it, nothing more, nothing less."

But even as a child, Barkley's personality seemed made of contradictory parts. As a youngster the combative part of his nature shared space with a much softer, more thoughtful side. At age eight, the self-described "wild child" knocked himself unconscious jumping from the roof of the projects while playing Superman. Yet his mother still described him as considerably "more serious" than "most boys his age."

"When something would happen that needed to be discussed, I could always sit down and talk to him like a man. That's what he always was, a little man. And when it came to our financial condition, he was always very understanding. He never wanted the kind of material things every other kid had. If I told him we didn't have money for something he asked for, he didn't get upset. He would just say, 'Okay, Momma.'"

Today, Barkley says, "I knew we were poor, but in that there was no shame." Secure in his family's love, "you could never have told me that our family was in need of anything. Not one thing."

As difficult as it may be to believe today, other children regarded Barkley as shy, and he was often the butt of teasing. Even in high school he seldom dated, showing much more interest in basketball than in girls. He was unflatteringly nicknamed "Big Head," and, according to his mother, "a lot of people called him a wimp." According to Charcey Mae, "the toughness he started to show in the NBA took me totally by surprise. The cursing, the fights, the running off at the mouth, I was not used to that kind of behavior by my Charles."

As he grew older, Charles took upon himself the responsibility for looking after his little brothers, Darryl and John. Most days, both his mother and grandmother worked, as he explained, "well into night," and he made sure that Darryl and John got home safely from school, prepared them something to eat, and, as he put it, tried to keep them from killing themselves or each other. He also made sure that the house was clean when his mother and grandmother arrived home. "It didn't make sense that my mother had to clean other people's houses all day and then come home and clean our house," he says. Each day, he mopped, swept, dusted, and polished—everything except wash dishes, which was the one chore he could not abide. Instead, they were stacked neatly in the sink. Even today, Barkley's extreme passion for neatness and cleanliness is the subject of much humorous commentary on the part of his teammates.

"Charles was the son who took over when I was gone," his mother says. "He became the

24

Charles Barkley was just "a typical sub" as a junior on the Leeds High School basketball team. But some of his skills were apparent early.

head of the house. . . . When it came to his two younger brothers, Darryl and John, he became their father figure. When I'd come home dead tired, he always told them, 'Leave Mom alone, she's tired.' But when I would get on them or punish them, he would always tell me to give them another chance."

Not that Charles was an angel. By the time he reached junior high school, he was, by his own description, "a petty thief" who amused himself by shoplifting inexpensive items from the handful of stores in Leeds. With a group of friends, he would lie in wait on Sunday night for the delivery trucks to drop off the week's supply of cakes and other goodies in front of the bakery and grocery store, then help himself to some sweets.

One night, disappointed with the flavors of the goodies that had been dropped off, Charles and his friends expressed their displeasure by engaging in a food fight, hurling cakes at one another and then converting the grocery carts to bumper cars. When the police arrived, the boys ran, with that giddy mix of fear and exhilaration, into the woods nearby. The police were soon left behind, but Charles, in a blind panic, "more scared that night than I had ever been in my life," ran face-first into a tree trunk, nearly knocking himself out.

Some of his friends graduated to more seriously criminal behavior—larceny, dealing marijuana—but Charles was, in his own words, "scared straight" by the episode. Mostly, it was the thought of his behavior shaming his mother and grandmother that motivated him to leave such foolishness behind. In addition to the embarrassment and hurt that his getting into real trouble would cause them, he knew that an arrest would likely interfere with his plans to go to college.

"Without basketball," claims Charles Barkley, "I probably would have wound up in jail. Probably not for anything major, but I would certainly have been caught eventually for some of the petty thefts I was committing. But when you're in jail, nothing's petty."

Basketball became an activity on which Charles could focus his restless energy, the basketball court a place where he could exorcise the pain he felt about his father's abandonment. (The infrequent contacts Charles had with his father, beginning at age nine, did little to repair their relationship. After his father failed to fulfill a promise to send his son a Christmas present one year, Charles vowed never to ask for or expect anything from him again. Today, the two maintain a cordial but distant relationship.)

Charles began playing ball at Leeds Elementary, the newly integrated grammar school that his mother and grandmother insisted he attend. Even though it was farther from his home than the all-black school, the formerly all-white Leeds Elementary had superior facilities and offered a better education than the other institution. Though Charles received a hostile reception from some of the white students—he was one of the first and few blacks to attend—and was criticized by other blacks for going to the white school, he has never regretted his decision. For the $30 she could ill afford, his mother also bought him a membership at the

Barkley drew double coverage in high school, even on an inbounds play.

Leeds Civic Center, where he could play basketball when school was not in session. Once again, Barkley was one of the first blacks to integrate the facility, and the team he played on as the center was mostly white. Despite some hostility, his experience there, as well as at Leeds Elementary, was mostly positive, and he "ultimately learned that you shouldn't judge people by their color or race."

By the time he reached junior high school, basketball "possessed" him. For a while, his enthusiasm exceeded his skills. He was short and pudgy; though a good ballhandler, he had a reputation as a shameless "gunner"—a selfish player who prefers to shoot rather than to pass—and was usually one of the last players chosen, if selected at all, for pick-up games. At first, he was not even good enough to make the team at Leeds Junior High, and when he did, he rarely got into games. As a tenth grader at Leeds High School, he was still just 5' 7", chubby, and less than special as a player. While the more talented sophomores played with the Leeds varsity, Charles was relegated to the junior varsity squad, where he still did not stand out. "Charles was an average player when he got to high school," his mother recalls, "not nearly as good as the other kids. . . . He was really too short for the team, but he had so much determination."

That determination both frustrated and motivated him. His mother remembers him returning home after games and practices to confide in his grandmother. "They just won't give me a chance," she remembers him saying. "I know I can play." Though sympathetic, his grandmother urged him to create his own opportunity: "Baby, just keep on working. If it's meant to be, you'll get your chance."

In the summer before Charles's junior year, he grew three inches. He also worked doggedly on his jumping, the one physical gift that he believed he possessed. He used a jump rope to strengthen his legs. "I thought he was going to jump that rope to death," his mother recalled. "He would jump and jump, jump, jump, jump, jump, jump. He did it for hours at a time."

He also invented his own exercise drill. "I knew I had to be stronger than the guys on the team," he said, "and I knew that I got my strength from my legs. I knew I had to be able to jump high and go until they all dropped from exhaustion. No matter how tired I got, I knew if my legs kept working, I could keep working." From a standing start, with both feet together— a vertical jump—he would leap the three-and-a-half foot tall chain link fence that bordered his family's property, then leap back again, over and over, "like a jumping jack," for hours on end.

Taller, stronger, he was a much improved player for his junior year. He was promoted to the varsity, but even though he grew another three inches in the course of the season, he was still, in his own words, "just another guy on a pretty good basketball team, a typical sub" who still needed a stroke of good luck to get any serious playing time and an opportunity to prove himself.

Then, late in the season, the team's second-best player, Austin Sanders, quit the squad at halftime of a game, following an argument with the coach. By default, Charles became a starter. On a talented team that went 26 and 3 before losing in the finals of the state championship, he was not needed to score much. So he concentrated on rebounding and discovered that he could outboard even much taller opponents. For the season, he averaged a more-than-respectable 13 points and 11 rebounds a game.

He continued to improve his play as a senior, although the difficulty of categorizing him as a player meant most college recruiters overlooked him when compiling their lists of the top collegiate prospects in the state. His 225 pounds seemed too much for his frame to carry, and at only 6'1" Barkley played center—even the guards on his team were taller than he. No college was especially interested in a "center in a guard's body," as Barkley described himself.

Those opinions started to change a little when Leeds took on Butler High School from Huntsville, Alabama. The game matched not only the two high schools in the state ranked number one in their respective classifications but pitted Barkley head to head with Huntsville's star 6'9" center, Bobby Lee Hurt. By consensus, Hurt was the best big man and top college prospect in the state. The confrontation was a mismatch. Barkley destroyed him, gathering 25 points and 20 rebounds in a Leeds win.

Charles went on to average 19 points and 18 rebounds a game—Leeds fans soon took to cheering his rebounds louder than his baskets—and his team went 26 and 3 again. Still, few schools showed much of an interest in him.

His particular combination of physical attributes and on-court skills just made him too unusual a player to project that he would be successful at the college level. College coaches were unwilling to believe that a player of his size could be a successful inside player.

Barkley initially committed himself to attend the nearby University of Alabama at Birmingham. UAB had never been a basketball powerhouse, but its unexpected success in the 1981 NCAA tournament convinced a number of top prospects to join its program. When Barkley learned that four starters from that squad were also returning, he recognized that the likelihood of his getting much playing time as a freshman was slim, so at the last minute he changed his mind and decided to attend Auburn University, some 100 miles southeast of Leeds.

Before Barkley, Auburn was one of the last colleges in the country a blue-chip basketball player would consider attending. Auburn played in the Southeastern Conference (SEC), where basketball ran a poor second to football in popularity. Of the SEC schools, only the University of Kentucky put much emphasis on basketball, and the level of hoops competition in the conference was not especially high. And even by the SEC's standard, Auburn's basketball program was shabby: At the time Barkley enrolled, the school had not had a winning season in six years and had never been to the NCAA tournament. In its home auditorium, the team regularly played in front of more empty seats than paying customers, drawing an average of only 5,300 fans per game to its 13,000-seat arena, even though tickets cost just a dollar.

For those few fans, there was little reason to

While Barkley guarded the middle, other players tended to pull up short and have their shots blocked.

believe that Barkley would be the player to turn the Auburn program around. He reported for his first practice as a freshman at 250 pounds, and in the course of the season he ballooned to above 270. The excess weight was more apparent because then, as today, Barkley disliked lifting weights.

As far as the team's coach, Sonny Smith, was concerned, his new recruit was both too short and too heavy. He saw little reason to expect that Barkley would be able to hold his own as a front-court player against much taller and more highly regarded players such as the University of Alabama's prize recruit Bobby Lee Hurt (despite the outcome of their high school duel), let alone the vaunted frontliners of top-dog Kentucky, 7'0" center Melvin Turpin and 6'8" jumping jack Kenny Walker.

Angered by Barkley's seeming lack of interest in consistently practicing hard—a shortcoming that the player freely owns up to even in the present day—Smith sought to motivate him through humiliation and abuse. He screamed at him constantly in front of his teammates, cursing him, berating him for his excess weight. By the coach's own admission, "I dog-cussed him, is what we would have called it where I come from."

Like all coaches, Smith wanted all his players to practice hard every day. Barkley, however, rose only to competitive challenge on the court. For example, when matched head-to-head in a scrimmage situation against Darrell Lockhart, the team's best returning player, Barkley was unstoppable, dominating Lockhart in every phase of the game. But in going through drills and repetitive exercises, he was lackadaisical.

One day, Hubie Brown came to visit a practice. Brown was one of the NBA's most respected head coaches, renowned as a no-nonsense disciplinarian and a master tactician. He fell into conversation with Smith's assistant, Tevester Anderson. Brown remembers Anderson complaining to him about their new player, "the fat one. He won't practice. He's lazy. He's a terrible example for our other kids. I can't do a thing with him."

Then, Brown recalled, Smith organized a freshmen-against-varsity intrasquad scrimmage: "On one play the kid comes down on a fast break. Off the dribble now, he throws the ball off the backboard, swoops in—the ball's at the top of the square now, easily 11 feet off the floor. He catches it, cups it in his hand, and—what!—throws it down. All in one motion!"

Stunned, Brown watched as "the kid"—who, he soon learns, is named Charles Barkley—gets 25 points and 20 rebounds in 25 minutes for an easy freshmen win over the varsity team. "My advice to you, my man," Brown told Anderson, "is to get to like the kid. We got a lot of guys in our league who can't do that."

3

THE ROUND MOUND OF REBOUND

Once the Auburn season began, it proved fairly easy for Barkley's coaches to follow Brown's advice. Though Barkley and Smith would never fully resolve their differences, no one could fail to appreciate Barkley's play in games. Teammates, opponents, coaches, fans, broadcasters—none had ever seen a player like Barkley, with his peculiar mixture of size, strength, and quickness. "No matter what I weighed," Barkley says, "I was always quick, and quickness was the key to my game. . . . When I keep my feet moving on the offensive end of the floor, there aren't many big guys who can keep up with me."

And Barkley was strong. Smith recalls that in practice Barkley loved to dunk with enough force to snap the breakaway rims on the baskets, probably because it brought practice to a halt. After Smith instituted a rule forbidding

At Auburn University, Barkley's weight was always an issue—for other people. Here he elevates to block a shot by the University of Alabama's Buck Johnson during the 1983 S.E.C. tournament.

such activity, Barkley dunked so ferociously that he dislodged the hoop from its moorings, which were anchored by twin cement blocks weighing 300 pounds apiece. Stomping and fuming, Smith ordered the team to help him fix the basket, but Barkley gently moved him out of the way and singlehandedly moved both blocks himself, fixed the basket, and then moved the 600 pounds of cement back into place. "It was an unbelievable physical feat," Smith remembers.

But Barkley's most significant physical feats took place on the basketball court during games. Smith would not start him in games immediately, hoping thereby to teach the freshman a lesson about approaching practice more seriously. Still, by the seventh game of the season the coach had no choice but to start him.

The previous game had been against the University of Tennessee, whose center, Howard Wood, was regarded as one of the conference's best players. Coming off the bench, Barkley, in his coach's words, "kicked [Wood's] tail somethin' bad that night. That's when it all started for Charles. From that point on, he was quite a legend in the SEC."

That game brought out another side of Barkley as well, for despite his fine play, Auburn suffered its first loss of the season. Afterwards, Barkley cried openly in the locker-room, much to the amusement of one of the upperclassmen on the team, whose experience at Auburn had left them more accustomed to defeat. "Man, you'd better not be crying around here after every loss," a teammate warned. "You'll flood us out of here."

Barkley never lost his hatred of losing, and it

was this hatred, as much as any of his physical skills, that propelled him to such heights on the court. At the end of the season, Auburn's unremarkable 14 and 14 record, which left them seventh in the conference, nonetheless constituted its best mark in years. Barkley became the first freshman in history to lead the SEC in rebounding, the first of a record three straight years in which he would do so. Yet he saw no reason to celebrate: "I thought we had had a pitiful season; I was embarrassed," he recalled. He felt the same way the next year after the Tigers improved by only one game, to 15 and 13, even though he again led the conference in rebounds, shot a phenomenal .644 from the floor, and scored more than 14 points a game while taking fewer than 9 shots a contest.

Those last three statistics point to one of the most important facets of Barkley's game: his unselfishness. Later on, his teams would rely on him to be their primary scorer, a responsibility he was more than able to fulfill, but at Auburn he was genuinely uninterested in scoring except to the extent that his team needed him to do it. He got most of his points off putbacks, finishing the break, or at the foul line, rarely off plays designed to get him the ball or allow him to go one-on-one. Smith marveled at his willingness and ability to do whatever the team needed in order to win, whether it be score a critical basket, nab a crucial offensive rebound, lead the fast break, or even set up a teammate with a perfectly executed pass.

Barkley also had an uncanny knack for the timely steal, blocked an inordinate number of shots for someone his size, and intimidated opponents with his relentlessly physical style.

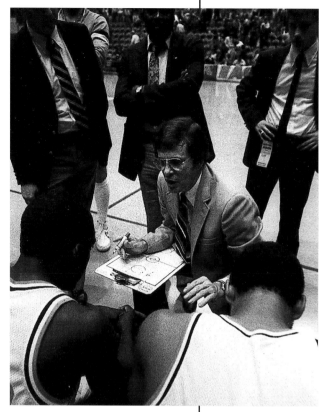

Coach Sonny Smith later admitted that he treated Barkley too harshly.

"When a guy comes down the lane, I want him to be wondering what side I'm going to hit him on," Barkley later explained to talk show host Charlie Rose.

Auburn became a flamboyant, dangerous team. On one night, they were capable of beating top-ranked Kentucky by 19 points (as they did during Barkley's junior year) and on another of losing to the league doormats. As Barkley's play and personality began to attract national attention, Auburn's publicists began to center on him as a means of drawing media interest to the university's basketball program. Unfortunately, they decided to focus on his weight as the best means of creating an image for him. In response, the press caricatured Barkley as a constantly ravenous devourer of junk food, urged him to pose for photographs while scoffing down slices of pizza and fried chicken, and hung a succession of denigrating nicknames on him, such as Boy Gorge, the Bread Truck, the Leaning Tower of Pizza, the Mouth of the South, the Doughboy, and the longest-lasting, the Round Mound of Rebound.

Believing that it would help the university, Barkley cooperated with this promotional angle, though he has since come to believe that he was exploited in allowing himself to be promoted as "an overweight freak. . . . I was the best player in the SEC for three years straight between

1981 and 1984, but the only thing anyone cared about was how many pizzas or chickens I could eat." Smith agrees, saying that if he had it to do over, he would treat Barkley much differently, including "not promot[ing] him as a fat kid." Of the nicknames, Barkley found only "the Round Mound of Rebound" not insulting.

Fed up with Smith's abusive tactics, Barkley actually quit the team and left the university for a brief time before the start of his junior season. He explained that in order for him to return to the team the coach would have to agree to treat him "like a person, not just a basketball player." Smith agreed. The screaming stopped, along with the insults about Barkley's weight and approach to practice, and Smith, in his own words, "never had any problems with him" again. "I was kind of stupid," the coach later admitted about his initial treatment of Barkley.

Along with the relationship between its head coach and star player, Auburn's play improved greatly in Barkley's junior year as well. The team recruited Chuck Person, a 6'8" forward with a tremendous shooting touch from long range who would also star in the NBA for many years. With Barkley unselfishly dominating the paint and Person, who became known as the Rifleman, firing away from outside, Auburn possessed a lethal inside-outside combination. After the most successful regular season in the school's history, the Tigers advanced to the championship of the SEC postseason tournament, where they lost to hated Kentucky by two points when Kenny Walker swished a desperation 18-foot jumper at the buzzer. "When we lost the SEC championship," Smith remembered, "Charles just sat on the floor on the other end of

Barkley took Auburn to its greatest basketball success-es. But in their biggest game—the S.E.C. champi-onship game in 1984—the University of Kentucky just managed to win. Barkley found the going tough as he tried to squeeze between Dickey Beal (11) and Melvin Turpin.

the arena and cried. He sat there for five min-utes and cried like a baby. I'd never seen any-thing like that before."

Auburn, still reeling from the loss, then was upset by the University of Richmond in the first round of its first-ever appearance in the NCAA tournament. Certain that he had little more to learn as a college player, Barkley opted to forego his senior season and declare himself eligible for the NBA draft. Building on the start Barkley had given it, Auburn enjoyed a few more successful years, anchored by Person and Chris Morris, another future NBA player, but with Barkley's departure, a special era in the history of Auburn basketball had come to an end. Smith put it simply: "Charles Barkley was Auburn basketball. He turned the entire program around by himself."

4

MIXING IT UP UNDERNEATH

Before becoming a pro, Barkley would have one more encounter with a hard-driving college coach. As the head man at Indiana University, Bobby Knight had earned a reputation as perhaps the loudest, most aggressive, most demanding, most abusive, and possibly the best coach in college basketball. As a tribute to his stature, he was asked to head the basketball team that would represent the United States at the 1984 Summer Olympic Games in Los Angeles, California.

Players invited to the tryouts included Patrick Ewing of Georgetown University, Chris Mullin of St. John's University, and Michael Jordan of the University of North Carolina. Each had been consensus All-Americans and won at least one award as the collegiate player of the year.

Though Barkley received an invitation to the Olympic Trials, it seemed unlikely that he would

---

The Philadelphia 76ers drafted Barkley hoping he would learn from all-time great Julius Erving and eventually take over Dr. J's role on the team.

overly impress Knight. He had not been selected either a first-, second-, or third-team All-American. The coach was the staunchest of basketball fundamentalists, and to many hoops traditionalists Barkley's very existence was an affront to their sensibilities. Knight, for example, seemed personally offended by Barkley's weight. "Have you ever coached a player that heavy?" a reporter asked him. "Not for long," Knight immediately quipped.

The General, as some called Knight, had hoped that Barkley would report for the Trials weighing 215. Instead, Barkley reported at 284 pounds, his heaviest weight ever. On the court, though, the poundage proved irrelevant, as Barkley quickly overwhelmed his fellow Olympic aspirants with his skills.

"Don't let him tell you that none of us stood out at the Trials," says Joe Dumars. "He did."

Steve Alford, star guard for Coach Knight at Indiana, agrees with Dumars. "He was definitely one of the top five guys there in terms of talent. . . . If any of us hadn't heard of Charles before the Trials, we certainly heard of him during and after the Trials. The thing that shocked everybody was that a man weighing 284 pounds could get up and down and off the floor quicker than anybody." Michael Jordan "was frankly amazed" by Barkley.

"I had never seen him play, only heard about him," Jordan recalls. "He was very creative, an unbelievable player. No one thought somebody with that type of body could do the things he did."

At the Trials, Barkley often guarded Jordan, but Jordan was rarely assigned to Barkley on the defensive end, because, as even the ultracompetitive Jordan is forced to admit, "I couldn't control him."

Like Jordan, Barkley used innovative methods on the court, but though the results he achieved were just as spectacular, the coaching staff was far less tolerant of his approach. Barkley refused to let the traditional wisdom about what a player of his size and position should be doing on the court confine his game. Instead of throwing an outlet pass after gathering a rebound, Barkley often dribbled the ball upcourt himself. In a halfcourt situation, he defied Knight by posting up inside, instead of staying on the perimeter.

Coach Bobby Knight cut Barkley from the 1984 Olympic team partly because he did not like Barkley's attitude.

According to Patrick Ewing, Barkley was far and away the best player at Bloomington. Alvin Robertson, then of the University of Arkansas and later a star guard with the San Antonio Spurs of the NBA, said that every time the players heard the rim snap from the force of a dunk, they would stop play and turn to see who had done it. Invariably, it was Barkley. Unfortunately, according to Robertson, Barkley's very success seemed only to antagonize Knight, as if every bucket he scored or created was further demonstration that the player knew better than the coach: "The coaches would get mad at him because he would dribble the ball, break the press, whatever it took to score."

"He certainly should have been on the team," believes Michael Jordan, who says that he does not know why Knight wound up cutting Barkley. Like many, however, he suspects that

Barkley's wisecracks and irreverence may have sealed his fate with the General. Knight, who continually harangued the players about the necessity of being on time for practice and meetings, was himself 15 minutes late for an evening chalktalk. "Hey, where the hell have you been?" Barkley shouted at Knight as the coach made his belated entrance.

Barkley claimed not to be overly upset by Knight's decision. His superb play at the Trials was well publicized. Mark Heisler, basketball writer for the *Los Angeles Times,* estimated that Barkley's worth in the upcoming NBA draft escalated $250,000 with each day of his performance at the Trials.

The Philadelphia 76ers used their fifth pick in the first round to draft him. The first four players selected—Hakeem Olajuwon of the University of Houston, Sam Bowie of Kentucky, Jordan of North Carolina, and Sam Perkins also of North Carolina—had all been much more highly touted as college players than Barkley. Philadelphia was a much better squad than the teams which had the first four picks. They were perennial doormats while the 76ers were a powerful, veteran unit that had won the NBA championship in 1983 and advanced to the Eastern Conference finals in the most recently concluded season. Although injuries and age were slowly taking their toll on the 76ers, the team's top five was still one of the most formidable in the game: the legendary Julius Erving and defensive stalwart Bobby Jones at forward; 12-time All-Star Moses Malone at center; Maurice Cheeks, at point guard; and the player Barkley would come to regard as the most talented of all of them, Andrew Toney, at the shooting guard.

On the surface, Barkley and the 76ers seemed a perfect match. A player desperate to win was joining a team accustomed to winning; the rookie would bring energy and enthusiasm to a team of veterans with infinite basketball wisdom to impart. As a creative young player with immense skills and perhaps a slight need for some emotional maturity, Barkley could spell and learn from Erving, an equally unconventional and talented player who had earned at least as much respect for his poise, leadership, dignity, and class as he had for his soaring flights to the basket. Barkley, it was hoped, was to be the bridge between past and future generations of greatness for a 76ers team fortunate enough to obtain a player of his caliber in the draft without having first plunged to the bottom of the league standings.

It did not quite work out that way. In Barkley's rookie season, 1984–85, the 76ers won 58 games—six more than the year before—and advanced to the semifinals of the Eastern Conference playoff. While clashing, in typically headstrong fashion, with head coach Billy Cunningham over practice habits, Barkley nevertheless worked his way into the starting lineup with his strong play.

In his career to that point, Barkley had never been his team's "go-to guy"—that is, the player his teammates "go to" (try to get the ball to) when the team most desperately needs a basket. But in the NBA, the full range of Barkley's skills became evident. The professional game is both much faster and much more physical than the college game, which made Barkley's unique combination of power and quickness that much more devastating. As a rookie, Barkley averaged

The 76ers never enjoyed the level of success expected of them. Here Barkley sits alone on the bench after the Milwaukee Bucks ousted the 76ers from the 1986 playoffs.

14 points—equal to his average over three seasons at Auburn—and almost 9 rebounds per game, in less than 30 minutes per contest. Though Jordan and Olajuwon beat him out in the Rookie-of-the-Year voting, he was named to the league's first team All-Rookie squad.

Realizing that Barkley could be as dominant an offensive player as he was a rebounder, Philadelphia began grooming him to take over from the aging Erving and Malone as the team's go-to guy. In his second season, playing 36 minutes a game, Barkley's scoring average climbed all the way to 20 points a game, second on the team only to Malone. Even more incredibly, Barkley snatched 13 boards a game—outrebounding the 6' 10" Malone, who is the NBA's fifth leading rebounder of all time. Malone, who was regarded as the league's dominant center and had won the MVP award three times, had just the year before led the NBA in rebounding for the fifth time in his illustrious career.

Barkley's remarkable feat placed him second in the league's list of top rebounders. The next season, 1986–87, his third in the league, he claimed the rebounding crown for his own, with 14.6 per game. That year, he also upped his scoring, to 23 points per game, while shooting almost 60 percent from the floor. For the first time, he was selected to play in the league's annual All-Star game, the first of nine consecutive appearances he was to make in the midseason classic. For the second straight year, he was voted All-NBA second team; he would go on to be voted All-NBA first or second team for ten consecutive seasons.

In 1986, 1987, and 1988, Barkley received the Schick Award, which uses a complex statistical formula to determine the player who has made the greatest all-around contributions to his team's success. "There's only a few guys great enough so they don't really have any special position," he said. "Magic [Johnson], Michael Jordan, and me."

5

DOWN LOW

There was one major problem with the way Barkley's career was developing, however: While he was improving, his team was not. The 58 wins the 76ers notched in his rookie season was the most the squad would win in his eight years in Philadelphia, and while Barkley was with the 76ers they would never advance deeper into the playoffs than the Eastern Conference semifinals. Meanwhile, through the 1980s, Larry Bird's Boston Celtics or Magic Johnson's Los Angeles Lakers played for the NBA championship every single year. By the end of that decade, the Detroit Pistons, who had traditionally been one of the NBA's worst teams, had become the league's best, losing in the finals in 1988 before winning the championship in 1989 and 1990. In the new decade, Jordan's Chicago Bulls, another former league doormat, took their turn at the top of the NBA heap, claiming

Advertisers loved Barkley's public image. One sneaker manufacturer created an ad campaign about Barkley playing one-on-one against Godzilla.

three consecutive titles in 1991, 1992, and 1993.

The stars of those teams were honored accordingly: In the first nine years Barkley was in the league, Jordan, Johnson, and Bird each won three Most Valuable Player Awards. More importantly, their talents were spotlighted in the league's most glittering showcases, the conference finals and championship round playoff series. For Johnson, Jordan, and Bird, their heroics at the most critical junctures of these absolutely crucial games were a large part of what had made them hoop legends, basketball immortals: Magic's 42-point performance at center as a rookie in the 1980 finals and his buzzer-beating "junior skyhook" to beat the Celtics in Game 4 of the 1987 finals; Jordan's all-time playoff record 63 points against the Celtics, 246 points in the 1993 finals, and 35 points and six three-pointers in the first half of the first game of the 1992 finals; Bird's all-around play—passing, rebounding, and scoring—in the 1984 and 1986 finals.

But the 76ers never played in such crucial games. Age and mismanagement demolished the veteran team that Barkley had joined, and similar miscalculations prevented the 76ers from being rebuilt to championship caliber. When Barkley joined the 76ers, Erving's best years were behind him; though still a superb player in many ways, his productivity steadily declined until his retirement following the 1987 season. Although his exit was as graceful as his play had been, the notoriously difficult Philadelphia fans seemed to resent Barkley, as if he had somehow hastened their idol's descent into athletic old age. Andrew Toney, who in his prime had been arguably the league's best shooting guard, suffered a series of debilitating foot injuries that rendered him, for the four years he played with Barkley, almost completely ineffective. Bobby Jones retired after the 1986 season.

And then there was Moses. Even with the decline of Erving, Toney, and Jones, a front line pairing Barkley and Malone would have been one of the league's most formidable, and with Maurice Cheeks in the backcourt Philadelphia would still have been a consistent contender. But on June 16, 1986, "the worst day in the Sixers' history," according to Barkley, Philadelphia traded Malone, underrated power forward Terry Catledge, and two valuable first-round draft picks to the Washington Bullets for center Jeff Ruland and forward Cliff Robinson. On that same fateful day, the 76ers, who were fortunate enough to possess the first pick in the entire college draft despite being a playoff team, traded that selection to the Cleveland Cavaliers for forward Roy Hinson.

The two trades proved disastrous. Had Philadelphia kept the first pick in the draft, they would have used it to draft Brad Daugherty, an extremely talented frontline player who with his passing skills and soft shooting touch would have perfectly complemented Barkley and either Malone or Ruland. Instead, Daugherty went to Cleveland, where he made the All-Star team five straight years and helped transform the Cavaliers into one of the league's top teams. Unnerved by the pressure of justifying the high cost Philadelphia had paid for him, Hinson, meanwhile, flopped as a 76er and was traded eighteen months later. As a 76er, Ruland played

As the 76ers team declined, Barkley became angry and demanded a trade.

a total of just 116 minutes in 5 games before a knee injury forced him to retire. Robinson, meanwhile, turned out to be an oft-injured one-dimensional gunner with little interest in rebounding or passing.

So Philadelphia's management had somehow managed to parlay the league's potentially best frontline into next to nothing. "Let's put it like this," Barkley once said when asked to analyze the trades in retrospect: "With a front line of me, Daugherty, and Moses, we'd have had a couple of championship rings by now. Who would have stopped us?"

In 1986–87, the team won just 45 games, down from 54 the season before. In 1987–88, the 76ers managed just 36 wins and failed to make the playoffs for the first time in 13 years, even though Barkley had perhaps his all-around best season, averaging a career-high 28 points a game, along with 12 rebounds. Led by Barkley, the team clawed its way back to the top of the Atlantic Division standings in 1989–90, only to be ripped apart again by another series of bad deals. By 1992, the 76ers had dropped to 35 wins and were again out of the playoff picture.

By that time as well, Barkley wanted out of Philadelphia. Through eight seasons with the 76ers, he had averaged 23.3 points and almost 12 rebounds per game, while shooting an extraordinary 58 percent from the floor. He was, without doubt, clearly the game's best forward, if not its best player. He played each and every game with a passion equal to his skills, which revealed itself in frequent outbursts of joy and anger. Sacrificed in service to an organization that, in his opinion, did not share his commitment to winning, his body was breaking down, and severe injuries to his shoulder, knees, and back had already made inroads on his talent. To show for it, he had no championship rings and had played in just 51 playoff games. By contrast, his best friend in the game, Jordan, had two rings and had played in 91 playoff games; Bird had three rings and had competed 164 times in the playoffs; Johnson had five rings and had been in 186 playoff games.

Never one to hide his feelings, Barkley displayed his frustration in numerous ways. An extremely emotional and vocal player under the best of circumstances, he annually appeared among the league leaders in technical fouls. He missed no opportunity to publicly criticize the Philadelphia ownership for its blundering. Occasionally, he extended this criticism to his teammates, particularly those whom he felt were giving less than their best effort. He even fought with the fans, chiding the Philadelphia faithful for their lack of support, occasionally responding to the taunts and catcalls of boobirds with obscene gestures and curses of his own.

For the most part, his excesses were tolerated. Teammates knew him to be as unselfish, on and off the court, as he was emotional, and his criticism was usually necessary and right on target. Rookies and lowly-paid benchwarmers always could find a home with Barkley. "In Philadelphia, Barkley took in new players like stray pets," sportswriter David Casstevens wrote. The outspokenness and outbursts of anger, as manifested in technical fouls and skirmishes with fans, were regarded as an inseparable part of the character that made him so extraordinary a player. "If you take away the emotion that fuels his game, he will no longer be Charles Barkley," Paul Westphal explains. "If you expect him to accept the challenges that he does, then you have to take some of the less-than-positive things that go with it."

"I don't have a bad temper except during games," Barkley says. And despite his often negative comments about fans, he remained one of the league's most popular players. "People respect honesty," he explains. "I got a reputation for being controversial. I resent that. I am one of the few athletes in the world who is for real. I'm not phony. Fans respect me for giving my all and showing my emotion."

At times, however, Barkley went too far. One such occasion was the night of March 26, 1991, when the 76ers met the New Jersey Nets at the Meadowlands Arena in East Rutherford, New Jersey. Near the end of a very close, frustrating game, Barkley lost his temper with a fan who had been cursing him all night. He turned and spat in the heckler's general direction, but to his horror, he hit an eight-year-old girl instead. He was suspended by the league for one game, fined a large amount, and villified around the country in the media. Less well-publicized were his subsequent personal apologies to the girl, which she and her family graciously accepted, and his purchase for them of season tickets for the next season. The family even attended, at his invitation, a celebrity banquet held in his honor.

By his own account as well as others, Barkley

was genuinely ashamed of his action; his wife, Maureen, says that the episode is one of the defining moments of his life. A subsequent incident, which went unreported in the press, gives some indication of the kind of pressures that can give rise to such behavior. A fan encountered Maureen Barkley, who happens to be white, on the street, cursed her, called her a "nigger lover," and spat in her face. As longtime NBA player Glenn "Doc" Rivers has pointed out, in none of the quite justifiable concern expressed about the little girl Barkley spat on was it mentioned that through his own antisocial behavior the fan Barkley spat at had exposed Maureen Barkley to an unrelenting torrent of vulgarity, obscenity, and racial slurs.

In any event, by the close of the 1991–92 season, incidents such as these, combined with Barkley's dissatisfaction with the state of the 76ers, had convinced both player and management that it was time to part company. On June 17, 1992, just one day past the six-year anniversary of "the worst day in the Sixers' history," Philadelphia traded Barkley to the Phoenix Suns for center Andrew Lang, forward Tim Perry, and guard Jeff Hornacek.

6

SUNS

For Philadelphia, the trade was as negatively one-sided as the earlier ones involving Malone and Daugherty. Phoenix's president and chief executive officer, Jerry Colangelo, characterized it as a "slam dunk" for his team.

Barkley was overjoyed about more than just the change of scenery. Phoenix was an excellent team that had won 53 games the previous season and advanced to the Western Conference semifinals. With the Suns, Barkley would be joining three All-Stars—guards Dan Majerle and Kevin Johnson and forward Tom Chambers—on a high-scoring, fastbreaking, eminently entertaining team that experts believed needed only to add a top-notch rebounder and some physical and mental toughness in order to reach the league's top echelon.

Before joining the Suns, Barkley had a pre-

With the Phoenix Suns, Barkley got his greatest chance at a championship. But Scottie Pippen, Horace Grant, Michael Jordan, and the rest of the Chicago Bulls won their third NBA title in a row in 1993.

Charles Barkley reacted with joy after he hit a critical basket during the 1993 championship series. Even with no championship rings on his fingers, Barkley will always be remembered as a winner.

view of the pleasure of playing with topflight teammates when he was selected as a member of the so-called Dream Team, as the basketball squad representing the United States at the 1992 Summer Olympics in Barcelona, Spain, was known. For the first time ever, professional players from the NBA were allowed to play on the U.S. Olympic team. Barkley's teammates thus included Jordan, Johnson, Bird, Ewing, David Robinson, Scottie Pippen, Karl Malone, John Stockton, Chris Mullin, and Clyde Drexler. It was called the greatest basketball team ever assembled, but at the games themselves it was Barkley who was by far the team's outstanding player, leading the team in scoring as the United States easily claimed the gold medal. "The Olympics showed me that when I play with good players I was even better," Barkley said. "The game was so easy for me over there. When you play with good players the game is simple. The game is only hard when you play with bad players."

And he taught that lesson to the entire NBA in 1992–93. Barkley led Phoenix to a league-best 62 wins while averaging 25.6 points, 12 rebounds, and a career-high 5 assists a game. For the first time in his career, his brilliance was honored with the Most Valuable Player Award. "I can't explain the last year of my life. No one gets it this good," Barkley said after the season.

There was but one blemish on the season:

Phoenix did not win the championship. They played for the title, but even Barkley's spectacular play was not enough to get them by Jordan's Chicago Bulls, who defeated the Suns in six extremely hard-fought games to claim their third straight crown.

For Barkley, the loss was especially disheartening because it soon became apparent that this might have been his best and perhaps last real chance at claiming the NBA title. Slowed by the chronic back problems that had begun troubling him in Philadelphia, in 1993–94 he averaged only 21.6 points and 11 rebounds per game. He was able to suit up for just 65 games, his lowest total ever, and for the first time in his career as a collegiate or professional player, he shot below 50 percent from the field. An excellent team nonetheless, Phoenix still managed to win 56 games in the regular season, and in the opening games of the playoffs, Barkley seemed rejuvenated, torching the Golden State Warriors for 56 points in one contest and leading the Suns to a two games to none advantage over the Houston Rockets in the Western Conference semifinals.

Then Barkley's back began to pain him again, and Houston battled back. After six games, the series was tied, but Barkley had suffered an injury to his groin muscle as well. Though he later admitted "I was done after Game Six," a painkilling injection right before tip-off enabled him to take the floor for Game Seven, and two more at halftime allowed him to continue. But despite 24 points and 15 rebounds he was not the dominating force he needed to be. He limped noticeably, and his disheartened teammates played poorly. With a few seconds to go and

Houston up 10, his frustration boiled over and he was ejected after shoving Olajuwon. "This is not the way it is supposed to end for Charles Barkley," a Phoenix sportswriter wrote.

The Phoenix organization did the best that it could to support him, adding Danny Manning, regarded as one of the league's best all-around talents, to Barkley's already stellar supporting cast for the 1994–95 season. And although a still convalescing Barkley started the season slowly, Phoenix zipped out to the league's best record. Then, Manning tore his knee apart in a practice and was lost for the rest of the year. Phoenix's championship hopes died with him. They were ousted from the playoffs by a resurgent Houston Rockets team on its way to a second-straight championship.

The Suns made it back to the playoffs in 1996, only to fall short once again. Barkley took great satisfaction, however, in his being invited to play that summer on the U.S. Olympic basketball squad, which became known as Dream Team III.

Even though his teams have never won an NBA trophy, Barkley has won over all his detractors. Many would agree with Sir Charles's proud self-assessment: "There will never be another player like me. I'm the ninth wonder of the world."

STATISTICS

CHARLES BARKLEY

SEASON	TEAM	G	FGA	FGM	PCT	FTA	FTM	PCT	RBD	AST	PTS	AVG
1984-85	Phila	82	783	427	.545	400	293	.733	703	155	1148	14.0
1985-86	Phila	80	1041	595	.572	578	396	.685	1026	312	1603	20.0
1986-87	Phila	68	937	557	.594	564	429	.761	994	331	1564	23.0
1987-88	Phila	80	1283	753	.587	951	714	.751	951	254	2264	28.3
1988-89	Phila	79	1208	700	.579	799	602	.753	986	325	2037	25.8
1989-90	Phila	79	1177	706	.600	744	557	.749	909	307	1989	25.2
1990-91	Phila	67	1167	665	.570	658	475	.727	680	284	1849	27.6
1991-92	Phila	75	1126	622	.552	653	454	.695	830	308	1730	23.1
1992-93	Phx	76	1376	716	.520	582	445	.765	928	385	1944	25.6
1993-94	Phx	65	1046	518	.495	452	318	.704	727	296	1402	21.6
1994-95	Phx	68	1141	554	.486	507	379	.748	756	276	1561	21.6
1995-96	Phx	71	1160	580	.500	566	440	.777	821	262	1649	23.2
Totals		890	13,445	7393	.550	7454	5502	.738	10311	3495	20,740	23.3

G	games
FGA	field goals attempted
FGM	field goals made
PCT	percent
FTA	free throws attempted
FTM	free throws made
RBD	rebounds
AST	assists
PTS	points
AVG	scoring average

CHARELES BARKLEY
A CHRONOLOGY

1963   Born Charles Wade Barkley on February 20, in Leeds, Alabama

1981   As overweight, undersized center for Leeds High, outplays Bobby Lee Hurt, top recruit in state of Alabama, in head-to-head matchup

1981–84 Nicknamed Round Mound of Rebound, leads Auburn University basketball program to its most successful years; leads Southeastern Conference in rebounding three straight years

1984   Cut by Coach Bobby Knight of Indiana from U.S. Olympic Basketball team; selected by Philadelphia 76ers in first round of NBA draft

1985   Named to NBA All-Rookie team

1986   Wins Schick Award for all-around contributions to team's success for first of three straight years

1987   Leads NBA in rebounding at 14.7 per game; leads league in offensive rebounds for first of three straight years; named All-NBA second team for second consecutive season

1988   Named All-NBA first team for first of four consecutive years (and six overall)

1991   Wins MVP of NBA All-Star game

1992   Traded to Phoenix Suns; wins Olympic Gold Medal as member of U.S. basketball squad known as the "Dream Team"

1993   Wins NBA MVP award while leading Phoenix to the NBA finals

1996   Plays on Dream Team III

SUGGESTIONS FOR FURTHER READING

Barkley, Charles, with Roy S. Johnson. *Outrageous: The Fine Life and Flagrant Good Times of Basketball's Irresistible Force.* New York: Simon & Schuster, 1991.

Barkley, Charles, with Rick Reilly. *Sir Charles: The Wit and Wisdom of Charles Barkley.* New York: Warner Books, 1994.

Casstevens, David. *Somebody's Gotta Be Me: The Wide, Wide World of the One and Only Charles Barkley.* Kansas City: Andrews and McMeel, 1994.

George, Nelson. *Elevating the Game: The History and Aesthetics of Black Men in Basketball.* New York: Fireside, 1992.

Stauth, Cameron. *The Golden Boys: The Unauthorized Inside Look at the U.S. Olympic Basketball Team.* New York: Pocket Books, 1992.

ABOUT THE AUTHOR

Sean Dolan has a degree in literature and American history from the State University of New York. He is the author of many biographies and histories for young adult readers, including *Michael Jordan* in Chelsea House's Black Americans of Achievement series and Larry Bird in Basketball Legends.

INDEX

PICTURE CREDITS

Reuters/Bettmann: pp. 2, 16; AP/Wide World Photos: pp. 8, 10, 32, 38, 52, 56, 58; UPI/Bettmann: pp. 13, 21, 40, 43, 46, 48; Bob Moore Photography: pp. 18, 24, 26, 30; Courtesy Auburn University, 36.